Mega-Funny Division Stories

24 Rib-Tickling Reproducible Tales With Companion Practice Sheets

by Dan Greenberg

SCHOLASTIC
PROFESSIONAL BOOKS

New York • Toronto • London • Auckland • Sydney
Mexico City • New Delhi • Hong Kong • Buenos Aires

Cover design by Kelli Thompson and Gerard Fuchs

Interior design by Melinda Belter

Illustrations by Jared Lee

ISBN: 0-439-22727-5

1 2 3 4 5 6 7 8 9 10   40   08 07 06 05 04 03 02

Contents

How to Use This Book

And now, without further delay, we present *Mega-Funny Division Stories,* the one division book that manages to be both *fun* and *educational*—all at the same time. Our readers ask, "How do you do it?"

We start with some SOLID MATHEMATICAL CONCEPTS, add a generous dose of FUN, a dash of our world famous SECRET SPICES, and then of course, what would a division book be without several hefty dollops of GENUINE WEASEL JUICE? And there you have it! A book that'll tickle your funny bone, touch your heart, and stick to your mathematical ribs with some of the best math problems, exercises, and other materials that you'll find anywhere!

> **Fact:** Students can learn to master division from this book.
> **Fact:** This book will make learning more fun.
> **Fact:** When learning is more fun, students learn more.

From fundamental division concepts to basic facts to long division to division with 2- and 3-digit divisors, remainders, estimation, problem solving, mental math, fractions, and many other key concepts, this book leaves no aspect of mathematical division and its many conceptual offshoots uncovered.

Beginners should spend their time primarily in the first half of the book. The concept lessons will help them get a handle on what division really means. The facts lessons will provide a step-by-step way for students to get the basics. Once basic division facts are mastered, students can explore the middle part of the book. The multi-digit computation problems will reinforce what they've just learned. Use the final third of the book to focus on solving problems in familiar and unfamiliar situations.

This book has it all. But that's only the beginning. *Mega-Funny Division Stories* also answers such important questions as:

• *What do dogs really want?*[1] [p. 41]
• *Who is Johnny Diviso?*[2] [p. 24]
• *What is the future of gum in this country?*[3] [p. 56]
• *How good are cats at long division?*[4] [p. 29]

[1] More food, by most estimations.
[2] You don't want to know.
[3] Bright, but someday may run out of flavor.
[4] In a word, not too good.

Directions

1. Buy this book.
2. Open the book.
3. Check out the table of contents. Mathematical topics are organized in a sequence. Lessons get more mathematically advanced as the book progresses. The book starts by explaining the *idea* of division. It then moves on to basic division facts, division in its various forms (1-digit divisors, 2-digit divisors, and so on) as well as estimation, problem solving, fractions, decimals, and mental math.
4. Give the stories to your students. A companion practice sheet accompanies each of the 24 division stories. Answers to the problems appear at the back of the book.
5. Watch the fun begin!

A Pledge

The author and publisher of this book hereby make this pledge:
If your students don't find the lessons and problems in this book both rib-ticklingly entertaining and educationally useful . . . well then, they have no sense of humor!

Dan Greenberg

Name_____ Date_____

Chuck the Friendly

Queen Fiona the Fair had three children—Carl the Magnificent, Wanda the Powerful, and Chuck the Friendly.

"I'm magnificent," said Carl the Magnificent.

"I'm powerful," said Wanda the Powerful.

"Why can't I be magnificent or powerful?" asked Chuck the Friendly.

"Because you're friendly," said Queen Fiona.

One day the queen came to her three children with a difficult problem. "Your Uncle Waldo the Swine has given us a gift of 6 pigs," she said. "How can I divide this gift so that each of you 3 children will get the same number of pigs?"

"I have a magnificent plan," said Carl the Magnificent. "Divide them like this."

For Carl

For Wanda

For Chuck

"I have a powerful plan," said Wanda the Powerful. "Divide the pigs this way."

For Carl   For Wanda   For Chuck

"Here's my plan," said Chuck the Friendly. "I'm not sure if it's good or not."

For Carl   For Wanda   For Chuck

The Queen looked at the three plans and—lo and behold—Chuck's plan was better than magnificent. It was better than powerful. It was a plan that actually WORKED. It gave an EQUAL number of pigs to each child.

"You have done well, Chuck," said the Queen. "You have divided the pigs equally. For that I will hereby change your name to anything you like."

Chuck thought long and hard about this. It would be nice to be called "magnificent" or "powerful." But he wasn't really very magnificent or powerful. He was friendly. Chuck decided to keep the name Chuck the Friendly.

"That is a good choice," said the Queen.

It came to pass that one day Chuck the Friendly became the king. He and his wife, Queen Mary With the Splendid Hair-Do, ruled for many happy years.

Which just goes to show that sometimes it's better to be friendly than it is to be magnificent or powerful.

Name_____ Date_____

Chuck the Friendly

Divide each picture into the number of groups shown. Then write the answer.

1. Divide 8 pigs into 4 groups.

$8 \div 4 =$ _____

2. Divide 8 pigs into 2 groups.

$8 \div 2 =$ _____

3. Divide 12 crowns into 4 groups.

$12 \div 4 =$ _____

4. Divide 12 crowns into 6 groups.

$12 \div 6 =$ _____

5. Divide 16 apples into 4 groups.

$16 \div 4 =$ _____

6. Divide 16 apples into 8 groups.

$16 \div 8 =$ _____

7. Make up your own division problem. Draw a group of things on the back of this sheet. Then show how to divide them. Write a number sentence to describe your picture.

Name_____ Date_____

Suzy Sawyer, Paul Bunyan's Pal

You've heard of Paul Bunyan. He cut down forests all over the USA. Once those trees were cut, who sawed them down to size? Suzy Sawyer, that's who. Suzy roamed the land with her Trusty Blue Saw, looking for logs to cut. Whenever Paul Bunyan had a really tough problem, he called Suzy.

Suzy and the Big Tree

How tall was the Big Tree? Some folks said the Big Tree was a mile high. Others said it was taller. They all agreed the Big Tree was so tall it had its own weather. Down below, the Big Tree could be warm and sunny. Up above, it could be snowing up a blizzard! It took Paul a full year to cut down the Big Tree—and he worked 16 hours a day. Once he got the Big Tree down, Paul couldn't move it! He called Suzy. With her Trusty Blue Saw, she sawed the Big Tree into 12 big logs.

Then Suzy was ready to load an equal number of logs onto each wagon. How many logs did she load?

1. Suzy wanted to load the 12 logs onto 4 wagons. How many logs could she load on each wagon?

$12 \div 4 =$ _____

2. One of the 4 wagons broke a wheel. Suzy had to load 12 logs onto 3 wagons. How many logs should go on each wagon?

$12 \div 3 =$ _____

3. The horse pulling the third wagon got a rock in his foot. Then Suzy had to load 12 logs onto 2 wagons. How many logs should go on each wagon?

$12 \div 2 =$ _____

4. Suzy finally called Rent-A-Wagon. Now Suzy could have a total of 6 wagons. How many logs would she load on each wagon?

$12 \div 6 =$ _____

How Suzy Got Her Trusty Blue Saw

One winter, it got so cold that Suzy's campfire froze. The flames stopped moving and turned blue. The same thing happened to Suzy's trusty saw, too. During a cold spell, Suzy left her saw outside. When she came back, it had turned stone-cold blue. But Suzy's Trusty Blue Saw was hard as a rock, and it could cut through anything!

5. Suzy used her Trusty Blue Saw to cut 20 ounces of frozen water into 5 equal-sized pieces. How many ounces did each piece weigh?

$20 \div 5 =$ _____

6. How many ounces would each piece weigh if Suzy cut 20 ounces of frozen water into 4 equal-sized pieces?

$20 \div 4 =$ _____

7. Suzy used her Trusty Blue Saw to cut up a frozen campfire. The fire weighed 16 ounces. If she cut it into 4 equal pieces, how much did each piece weigh?

$16 \div 4 =$ _____

8. If Suzy cut a 21-ounce fire into 7-ounce pieces, how many pieces did she cut?

$21 \div 7 =$ _____

Name_____ Date_____

Suzy Sawyer, Paul Bunyan's Pal

Suzy and the Tree of Confusion

In the Confusion Forest, Paul cut down a tree so full of confusing knots that it gave him a headache just to look at it. He brought the tree to Suzy to straighten out. Every time she tried to straighten a knot, she got so confused that she had to start all over again. Finally Suzy hooked the tree over a rock, pulled with all her might, and kept her eyes closed so she wouldn't get confused. All the knots came out, leaving the tree as straight as an arrow. Then she cut the tree in pieces with her Trusty Blue Saw.

Solve these division problems.

1. Suppose Suzy cut the 18-yard-tall tree into 3 pieces. What was the length of each piece?

    $18 \div 3 =$ _____

2. Suppose Suzy decided to cut the tree into 6 pieces. That would change the size of each piece. How long would each piece be?

    $18 \div 6 =$ _____

3. Suppose Suzy wanted to cut the log into pieces that were 2 yards long. How many pieces would she have?

    $18 \div 2 =$ _____

4. Into how many 9-yard long pieces could Suzy cut the log?

    $18 \div 9 =$ _____

5. Make up your own Suzy Sawyer problem. Write it on the back of this sheet. Ask a friend to solve it.

Name_____ Date_____

Divisor, Quotient, Dividend

Divisor, quotient, dividend:
Three important words to remember, friend
It's like a train with a quotient caboose
The divisor's second, fast and loose
The engine's the dividend, out in the lead
Chugging ahead, picking up speed.

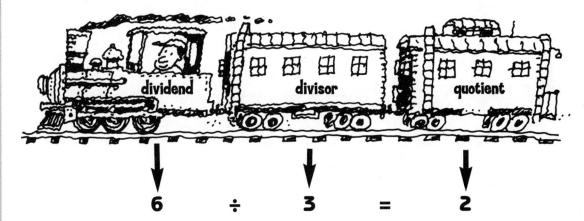

6 ÷ 3 = 2

Now sometimes people use a bracket to divide
It's like an L that's been turned on its side
Or a little doghouse with the divisor at the door
Inside is the dividend, sleeping on the floor.
On top is the quotient, enjoying the view
Dividing 6 by 3 gives a quotient of 2.

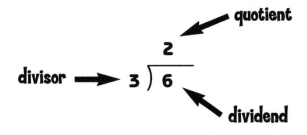

So that's the story, ladies and germs,
Never forget these three important terms:
Divisor, quotient, dividend.
Three important words to remember, friend.

Name_____ Date_____

Divisor, Quotient, Dividend

Complete these problems.

1. Circle the quotient in $8 \div 4 = 2$.

2. Circle the dividend in $15 \div 3 = 5$.

3. Circle the divisor in $9 \div 3 = 3$.

4. In $8 \div 2 = 4$, what is the quotient? _____

5. In $10 \div 5 = 2$, the 5 is the _____.

6. In $14 \div 2 = 7$, the 14 is the _____.

7. In $18 \div 6 = 3$, what is the divisor? _____

8. In $100 \div 20 = 5$, the greatest number is the _____.

9. Circle the dividend in $3\overline{)12}$ with quotient 4 .

10. Circle the divisor in $7\overline{)21}$ with quotient 3 .

11. Circle the quotient in $6\overline{)30}$ with quotient 5 .

12. In $8\overline{)48}$ with quotient 6 , what is the divisor? _____

13. In $10\overline{)200}$ with quotient 20 , 200 is the _____.

14. Add the quotients for $50 \div 2 = 25$ and $36 \div 6 = 6$.

    What sum do you get? _____

Name_____ Date_____

Professor Kingsley Invents Backwards Division

They called her dizzy,
They called her mad,
But Professor Bonita Kingsley
And her assistant, Chad,
Were working in the lab
One night late
When they made a discovery
That was truly great.
Kingsley was dividing
The number eighteen
When she found herself lost
In a mathematical dream.
When she awoke, Kingsley
Had this explanation:
"I've discovered how to divide,
Using just MULTIPLICATION!
We've done it, Chad,"
Kingsley added, grinning,
"This is only the start,
This is just the beginning!
This is really great!
This is really exciting!
We've discovered a BACKWARDS
Way of dividing!"

*To divide BACKWARDS
by multiplying,
try these examples.*

18 ÷ 3 = ?

**THiNK:
3 times what
number is 18?**

Answer: 6

9 ÷ 3 = ?
  3 times what number is 9?
                    Answer: 3

12 ÷ 2 = ?
  2 times what number is 12?
                    Answer: 6

15 ÷ 5 = ?
  5 times what number is 15?
                    Answer: 3

Name_____ Date_____

Professor Kingsley Invents Backwards Division

To solve these division problems—MULTIPLY!

1. $6 \div 2 = ?$ **THiNK**: 2 times what number is 6?   Answer: _____

2. $12 \div 4 = ?$ **THiNK**: 4 times what number is 12?   Answer: _____

3. $12 \div 6 = ?$ **THiNK**: 6 times what number is 12?   Answer: _____

4. $18 \div 2 = ?$ **THiNK**: 2 times what number is 18?   Answer: _____

5. $20 \div 4 = ?$ **THiNK**: 4 times what number is 20?   Answer: _____

6. $24 \div 3 = ?$ **THiNK**: 3 times what number is 24?   Answer: _____

7. $25 \div 5 = ?$ **THiNK**: 5 times what number is 25?   Answer: _____

8. $28 \div 4 = ?$ **THiNK**: 4 times what number is 28?   Answer: _____

Use backwards division to solve these problems.

9. Chad wants to divide 18 by 6. What two numbers
can he multiply to get the dividend? What is the quotient? _____

10. Professor Kingsley had to divide 24 by 6. What two numbers
can she multiply to get the dividend? What is the quotient? _____

11. To find a quotient, Chad multiplied 3 x 4. Write a division
problem that Chad might have been trying to solve. _____

12. Look at the circled numbers in these
division problems.
What do you notice to be true?

**HiNT:
Try multiplying the
circled numbers.**

$4 \div \boxed{2 = 2}$ $14 \div \boxed{2 = 7}$ $9 \div \boxed{3 = 3}$ $15 \div \boxed{3 = 5}$

_____

_____

Name_____ Date_____

Division Believe It or Not!

*Are these Fascinating Facts
too UNBELIEVABLE to be TRUE?
YOU be the judge!*

Believe It . . . or Not!

An **ANCiENT EGYPTiAN DOG** was able to solve **SUPER-HARD** division problems just by tapping its **PAW** on the **GROUND!** This **HiGHLY iNTELLiGENT** dog was one of the most **AMAZiNG CREATURES** that **EVER LiVED!**

Actually, the dog could solve any division problem—as long as the quotient was 6! When it was given any other kind of problem to solve, the dog would make a mistake. But if the quotient was 6, the pup never failed!

Solve the division problems below. Which problem would this SUPER POOCH have been able to solve correctly?

$10 \div 2 =$ _____ $2 \overline{)8}$ $4 \div 2 =$ _____ $2 \overline{)12}$

$9 \div 3 =$ _____ $3 \overline{)15}$ $6 \div 3 =$ _____ $3 \overline{)24}$

Believe It . . . or Not!

A man **STUCK iN A MONTANA CABiN** once lived on nothing but **DiViSiON PROBLEMS** for **ONE SOLiD WEEK!** "Tastes like **CHiCKEN!**" he said afterward.

Well, it wasn't actually a week. It was one day. And the man wasn't exactly stuck. But he did have NOTHING TO EAT—unless you count the 5-pound bag of corn chips he found in the cabin. It is not known how many corn chips he ate that day. But the bag was mysteriously EMPTY when he left!

Here are some problems that are good for controlling your appetite for division.

$16 \div 4 =$ _____ $8 \div 4 =$ _____ $4 \overline{)20}$ $4 \overline{)12}$

$5 \overline{)25}$ $5 \overline{)15}$ $30 \div 5 =$ _____ $10 \div 5 =$ _____

Name_____ Date_____

Division Believe It or Not!

Believe It . . . or Not!

A woman in Arkansas once **DEFEATED** a **DEADLY POISONOUS RATTLESNAKE** using only **DIVISION PROBLEMS** and her **BARE HANDS!**

Okay, it wasn't actually a deadly rattlesnake. It was a turtle. But turtles, like SNAKES, are REPTILES—and REPTILES can be DANGEROUS! This turtle measured over 10 centimeters in length (that's almost 4 inches)! The woman didn't actually USE the DIVISION PROBLEMS to FIGHT the BEAST, but she would have if it had been necessary!

Solve these UNBELIEVABLE division facts.

1. $14 \div 2 =$ _____

2. $2\overline{)6}$

3. $18 \div 2 =$ _____

4. $2\overline{)16}$

5. $12 \div 3 =$ _____

6. $3\overline{)21}$

7. $27 \div 3 =$ _____

8. $3\overline{)18}$

Believe It . . . or Not!

A young man in **FLORIDA** used **DIVISION** to earn exactly **ONE MILLION DOLLARS** in a single **DAY!**

Actually, he didn't earn the MILLION DOLLARS. He found it . . . in his pocket. And it wasn't a MILLION dollars. It was a hundred dollars he received as a birthday gift. "Without DIVISION, I might never have gotten this money," the young man said. "Then again," he added, "maybe DIVISION had NOTHING to do with it."

Solve MORE UNBELIEVABLE division facts.

9. $28 \div 4 =$ _____

10. $32 \div 4 =$ _____

11. $4\overline{)24}$

12. $4\overline{)36}$

13. $40 \div 5 =$ _____

14. $20 \div 5 =$ _____

15. $5\overline{)35}$

16. $5\overline{)45}$

Name_____ Date_____

The Five Things Millionaires Do That You Don't Do!

by William "Bill" Klepper

Hi, this is William "Bill" Klepper. Folks often ask me, "Bill, just what are the five things millionaires do that I don't do?" Usually, I just laugh, but then I got to thinkin' that I could write a BOOK about this. Here it is.

Step 1: Have parents with millions of dollars.
When I tell people this, they slap their foreheads. *"Of course!"* they cry. *"If only I'd thought of that!"* Well, they didn't think of it. *That's* why they don't have a million dollars!

Step 2: Have parents with BiLLiONS of dollars.
This is the real key to wealth. Think billions, not millions. Remember, the more money your parents have, the more you might get.

Step 3: Have friends or relatives who have millions of dollars.
The hard part is getting them to give you the money. Try begging. Sometimes it works.

Step 4: Once you have the money, keep it.
Millionaires hold on to their money, and so should you. The next time someone asks you for a million dollars, give them a couple of quarters instead.

Step 5: Know your division facts.
It's true—most millionaires and billionaires know their division facts. And so should you!

To get started, solve the problems below.

18 ÷ 6 = _____   30 ÷ 6 = _____   21 ÷ 7 = _____   14 ÷ 7 = _____

8)‾16‾   8)‾24‾   9)‾18‾   9)‾36‾

Name_____ Date_____

The Five Things Millionaires Do That You Don't Do!

Do you want to *feel* like a million bucks? Then solve these division problems!

1. $42 \div 6 =$ _____   **2.** $36 \div 6 =$ _____   **3.** $54 \div 6 =$ _____

4. $48 \div 6 =$ _____   **5.** $28 \div 7 =$ _____   **6.** $63 \div 7 =$ _____

7. $56 \div 7 =$ _____   **8.** $49 \div 7 =$ _____   **9.** $48 \div 8 =$ _____

10. $56 \div 8 =$ _____   **11.** $72 \div 8 =$ _____   **12.** $64 \div 8 =$ _____

13. $9 \overline{)54}$ **14.** $9 \overline{)72}$ **15.** $9 \overline{)63}$

16. $9 \overline{)81}$ **17.** $6 \overline{)12}$ **18.** $6 \overline{)24}$

19. $7 \overline{)35}$ **20.** $7 \overline{)42}$ **21.** $8 \overline{)40}$

22. $8 \overline{)32}$ **23.** $9 \overline{)27}$ **24.** $9 \overline{)45}$

Mega-Funny Division Stories Scholastic Professional Books

Name_____ Date_____

Nancy Nimms, Bargain Hunter

I, Nancy Nimms, am a professional bargain hunter. Some people hunt big game. I hunt Big Bargains. How good a bargain hunter am I? I once bought a $1,400 jacket for *11 cents!* How do I get such deals? One of my secrets is that I buy **TEN** of the same item at a time.

What if you don't need ten items? You buy them anyway! For example, here's a shoe bargain I got yesterday.

Bargain #1: Left Shoes

To get the absolute LOWEST price, I had to buy ten LEFT shoes. But don't worry. Next week RIGHT shoes will be on sale . . . I hope.

Figure out the price of each LEFT shoe.

Regular Price: **$50** for **10** left shoes: $50 ÷ 10 = $5 per shoe

Sale Price: **$40** for **10** left shoes: $40 ÷ 10 = _____ per shoe

Coupon Price: **$30** for **10** left shoes: $30 ÷ 10 = _____ per shoe

My Price: **$20** for **10** left shoes: $20 ÷ 10 = _____ per shoe

What a deal, eh? Hey, wait a minute. Do you notice a pattern in the problems above? Use the pattern to find the answers to the problems below. You may use a calculator.

1. 80 ÷ 10 = _____

2. 10 ÷ 10 = _____

3. 90 ÷ 10 = _____

4. 100 ÷ 10 = _____

Bargain #2: Shovels

Shopping is like hunting. You need to hide in the weeds. You need to wait until you flush out the bargains. Below are some bargains I got on **TEN** snow shovels. Now some folks say to me: *What are you going to do with ten snow shovels?* Not a problem, I say. I'll think of something . . . I hope.

Figure out the price of each shovel.

Regular Price: **$500** for **10** shovels: $500 ÷ 10 = $50 per shovel

Sale Price: **$400** for **10** shovels: $400 ÷ 10 = _____ per shovel

Coupon Price: **$300** for **10** shovels: $300 ÷ 10 = _____ per shovel

My Price: $200 for **10** shovels: $200 ÷ 10 = _____ per shovel

Do you see a pattern in the problems above? Use the pattern to find the answers to these problems. You may use a calculator.

5. 600 ÷ 10 = _____   **6.** 900 ÷ 10 = _____

7. 570 ÷ 10 = _____   **8.** 110 ÷ 10 = _____

Bargain #3: 1998 Calendars

Here's my big idea about shopping: *Buy now. Think later.* Now sure, this can cause problems. You can end up with too many snow shovels or left shoes. But think of all the money you save! Check out these deals I got on 1998 calendars. This time I had to buy 100 instead of 10.

Figure out the price of each calendar.

Regular Price: **$500** for **100** calendars: $500 ÷ 100 = $5 per calendar

Sale Price: **$400** for **100** calendars: $400 ÷ 100 = _____ per calendar

Coupon Price: **$300** for **100** calendars: $300 ÷ 100 = _____ per calendar

My Price: $200 for **100** calendars: $200 ÷ 100 = _____ per calendar

Once again, I see a pattern in the problems above. Find the answers to these problems. You may use a calculator.

9. 600 ÷ 100 = _____   **10.** 2,000 ÷ 100 = _____

11. 3,000 ÷ 100 = _____   **12.** 800 ÷ 100 = _____

Name_____ Date_____

Nancy Nimms, Bargain Hunter

Use your division skills to solve these problems.

1. $70 \div 10 =$ _____

2. $150 \div 10 =$ _____

3. $230 \div 10 =$ _____

4. $700 \div 10 =$ _____

5. $890 \div 10 =$ _____

6. $60 \div 10 =$ _____

7. $100 \div 10 =$ _____

8. $800 \div 10 =$ _____

9. $700 \div 100 =$ _____

10. $4,000 \div 100 =$ _____

11. $900 \div 100 =$ _____

12. $6,000 \div 100 =$ _____

Final Deal: Hey, I got a lot of bargains today. But you got the best deal of all— you learned something. Can you describe what you learned?

13. In your own words, write a rule for dividing by 10. How does your rule show a shortcut for dividing?

   _____

   _____

   _____

14. In your own words, write a rule for dividing by 100. How does your rule show a shortcut for dividing?

   _____

   _____

   _____

15. Think of a rule for dividing by 1,000. Try some examples using your rule. Does your rule work?

   _____

   _____

   _____

Name_____ Date_____

Johnnie Diviso, Division Detective

Today's Episode: Trouble in Noodle Town

My name is Johnette "Johnnie" Diviso. I'm a cop—
a tough cop. I work in the Division Division. Don't
laugh. The Division Division is the division where we
use *division* to solve crimes. Get it? I didn't think so.

Anyhow, I'm sitting in my office at the Division
Division. I'm doing a division problem: 42 divided by 3.

First, I write down the problem.
Then I ask myself: *How many
times does 3 go into the 4 in 42?*

It goes 1 time. I write down 1.
Then I multiply 1 by 3 to get 3.
I write down 3 and subtract.

Next I bring down the 2.
Then I ask myself: *How many
times does 3 go into 12?*

It goes 4 times. I write down the 4.
Then I multiply 4 by 3 to get 12.
I write down the 12 and subtract.

Just as I'm about to find the
quotient, the phone rings.
It's my boss, Victor Quotient.
"Diviso, get down here!" he roars.

I zip over to Captain Quotient's office. The captain introduces me to Mark Koogler, the owner of Noodle Town. It appears that 48 boxes of noodles were stolen!

"It's the biggest noodle heist in Noodle Town history," Koogler says. "Here's what we know: The crooks split the 48 boxes equally and drove away in 4 trucks."

"If we can find those trucks, we've got them," Quotient says. "But we need to know EXACTLY how many boxes of noodles were on each truck."

"Can you help me?" pleads Koogler.

"Hmm," I say. "Suppose I divided 48 by 4. That should tell us how many boxes were on each truck."

So I did the division. "There are 12 boxes on each truck," I told Koogler.

"Amazing!" Koogler said. "How did you do it so fast, Johnnie?"

"Easy," I said. "I used DIVISION."
Then I showed him the work
you see to the right.

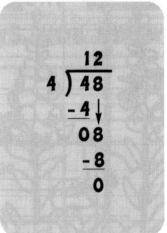

The rest, as they say, is history.
They found the trucks. They found the crooks.
They found the noodles. The greatest Noodle Heist in the history
of the city was solved.

"Thanks, Johnnie Diviso!" said a grateful Koogler.

As for Captain Quotient, did I detect a smile on his face?

"Nice work, Diviso," he said in his gruff voice. That's good enough for me.

Name_____ Date_____

Johnnie Diviso, Division Detective

I dare you to solve these division problems.

1. $2 \overline{)20}$ 2. $3 \overline{)33}$ 3. $2 \overline{)32}$ 4. $6 \overline{)30}$

5. $4 \overline{)40}$ 6. $5 \overline{)35}$ 7. $3 \overline{)63}$ 8. $4 \overline{)84}$

9. $2 \overline{)92}$ 10. $6 \overline{)72}$ 11. $7 \overline{)91}$ 12. $3 \overline{)57}$

13. $4 \overline{)96}$ 14. $3 \overline{)99}$ 15. $6 \overline{)84}$ 16. $8 \overline{)96}$

17. Captain Quotient has 3 detectives, including Johnnie. Last year the 3 of them were given a total of 51 cases. If each detective had an equal number of cases, how many cases were given to Johnnie?

_____

18. This year there were 64 cases for 4 detectives. How many cases did each detective cover?

_____

19. Johnnie found 96 pounds of money from a bank robbery. If she divides the money into 3 bags, how many pounds will each bag weigh? If she divides the money into 6 bags, how many pounds will each bag weigh?

_____

_____

20. Johnnie needs to keep a watch on a bank for 24 hours a day. If she splits the job with 5 other helpers, how many hours will each helper need to cover?

_____

Name_____ Date_____

Pierre LeDoo, Mountain Climber ("I Don't Like Heights")

I am Pierre LeDoo, one of the world's great mountain climbers. Does it matter that I do not like heights? I don't think so. Instead of HIGH mountains, I climb WIDE mountains.

Take a look at these two mountains. Anyone can climb a tall mountain. But a *wide* mountain is a real challenge!

**10,000 feet tall
Tall Mountain: Dull.**

**10,000 feet wide
Wide Mountain: Exciting!**

Suppose I put 3 climbers on a rope that is 46 feet long. If they are an equal distance from each other, how far apart will they be?

I divide 46 by 3 as I normally would. You see that I am left with a 1. This is the **remainder**. It is the amount of rope that is left over after I divide.

Each climber will be 15 feet away from each other— and 1 foot of rope will be left at the end.

$$
\begin{array}{r}
15\ \text{R1} \\
3\overline{)46} \\
-3 \\
\hline
16 \\
-15 \\
\hline
1 \\
\end{array}
$$

Name_____ Date_____

Pierre LeDoo, Mountain Climber

Remember: The remainder is the amount left over after division. Copy these problems. Find the quotient and the remainder for each problem.

1. $2\overline{)23}$ 2. $3\overline{)29}$ 3. $3\overline{)50}$ 4. $5\overline{)54}$

5. $4\overline{)49}$ 6. $5\overline{)62}$ 7. $4\overline{)58}$ 8. $6\overline{)76}$

9. $7\overline{)79}$ 10. $8\overline{)95}$ 11. $4\overline{)99}$ 12. $3\overline{)77}$

13. $5\overline{)96}$ 14. $6\overline{)89}$ 15. $7\overline{)88}$ 16. $8\overline{)97}$

Now solve these problems.

17. On Mt. Lowdown, I tied a rope that was 59 yards long to a pole. If I spaced 4 climbers evenly along the rope, how far apart were they? How many yards of rope was left over?

_____

18. Mt. Widebottom is 64 km wide. If I go across the entire width of the mountain in 5 days, how many kilometers would I cover each day? How many kilometers would be left over on the last day?

_____

19. Six climbers are spaced out evenly on a rope that is 58 feet long. How many feet of rope is left over?

_____

20. How many feet would you need to add to the rope in problem 19 in order to have no rope left over?

_____

Mega-Funny Division Stories Scholastic Professional Books

Name_____ Date_____

Cats and Division: What's the Connection?

The Cat Council wanted to know the answer to the following questions:

What do cats think of division?
How big a role does division play in their lives?

The council asked 100 cats about division.

How important is division in your life?

(A) Extremely important: It plays a huge role in my life.

(B) Somewhat important: I can take it or leave it.

(C) Unimportant: I'm a cat. I don't even know what division is!

How often do you use division in your daily life?

(A) All the time: I divide whenever I'm not prowling or snoozing.

(B) Sometimes: I use division whenever I need it.

(C) Never: I'm a cat. I don't even know how to divide!

How good are you at dividing 3-digit numbers?

(A) Excellent: I always get the correct quotient.

(B) So-So: I sometimes make mistakes.

(C) Terrible: I'm a cat! I don't even know how to hold a pencil!

Surprisingly, 100% of the cats in our survey chose C as their answers for the questions above.

To learn more about dividing 3-digit numbers, all cats should read the next page.

Dividing 3-Digit Numbers

Write down the problem.
Then ask: *How many times does 5 go
into the first digit, 2?*
Five doesn't go into 2, so ask:
*How many times does 5 go into
the first two digits, 23?*
It goes 4 times.

$$5\overline{)235}$$

Multiply 4 by 5 to get 20.
Write down the 20 and subtract.
Bring down the 5.
Then ask: *How many times does
5 go into 35?*
It goes 7 times.

$$
\begin{array}{r}
4 \\
5\overline{)235} \\
-20 \\
\hline
35
\end{array}
$$

Multiply 7 by 5 to get 35.
Write down the 35, and subtract.
The quotient is 47. There is no
remainder.

$$
\begin{array}{r}
47 \\
5\overline{)235} \\
-20 \\
\hline
35 \\
-35 \\
\hline
0
\end{array}
$$

Name_____ Date_____

Cats and Division: What's the Connection?

You don't have to be a cat to solve the following division problems.

1. $4 \overline{)132}$ 2. $2 \overline{)112}$ 3. $3 \overline{)216}$ 4. $4 \overline{)192}$

5. $6 \overline{)336}$ 6. $5 \overline{)465}$ 7. $7 \overline{)224}$ 8. $6 \overline{)576}$

9. $4 \overline{)852}$ 10. $8 \overline{)912}$ 11. $9 \overline{)621}$ 12. $3 \overline{)777}$

13. $8 \overline{)272}$ 14. $7 \overline{)686}$ 15. $6 \overline{)384}$ 16. $9 \overline{)432}$

17. A group of 136 cats split up into 4 groups. How many cats were in each group?

_____

18. A cat eats 6 ounces of food each day. How many days will it take the cat to finish a 252-ounce bag of cat food?

_____

19. Winky the cat runs at a speed of 7 meters per second. How many seconds will it take Winky to run 112 meters?

_____

20. Jamie takes her cat Snookums for a walk once a week. How many walks does Snookums take in a 365-day year? Suppose Jamie decides to give Snookums a walk once every 6 days. How many more walks will Snookums take over a year's time?

_____

Name_____ Date_____

Adventures in Division

Part I: A Division Timeline

The story of division is long and interesting. Here are some of the UNBELIEVABLE highlights along the way.

Solve the problems on the timeline.

443 B.C. The Greek philosopher Dividicus first thinks about division when he divides a cheese pie. Curiously, he gives himself a larger piece than his pals! Needless to say, no one is impressed with this unequal form of dividing.

1. The actual cheese pie divided by Dividicus weighed 77 ounces. If Dividicus had divided it equally, how many ounces should he and each of his 6 friends have gotten? _____

410 B.C. Ancient Chinese mathematician Quo Shun invents division as we know it today. Dividing becomes the rage in ancient China. Everyone does it! Then the fad mysteriously ends. Division is forgotten for hundreds of years.

2. Quo Shun's quotient for an early division problem was 8 R2. The number she divided by (the divisor) was 4. What number did Quo Shun divide? _____

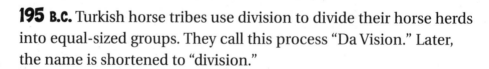

195 B.C. Turkish horse tribes use division to divide their horse herds into equal-sized groups. They call this process "Da Vision." Later, the name is shortened to "division."

3. A Turkish chief divided his herd of 258 horses into 6 groups— 1 group for each sub-chief. How many horses did each sub-chief get? _____

Mega-Funny Division Stories Scholastic Professional Books

62 B.C. The Romans use division to conquer the world. "Divide and Conquer" is the slogan of the Roman generals as they move across battlefields, taking no prisoners and no remainders.

4. Experts say that the Roman army presented its enemies with this choice: *Divide to solve this problem, or we will conquer you!* Suppose an army of 872 soldiers split up into 9 groups. What would be the best way to organize the groups? How many soldiers would be in each group? _____

127 A.D. The Dark Ages begin. All division is forgotten. No one has the foggiest idea how to divide things anymore.

5. Although division is completely lost, multiplication survives the Dark Ages. How can you use multiplication to find the quotient of 556 ÷ 8? _____

844 A.D. Division is now against the law in many places. Groups meet in underground caves to divide in secret. They make a lot of mistakes in their division because the cave is very dark and they forget to bring torches.

6. A Secret Group divides a Secret Number by 6. Then it divides the quotient by 6 to get a final quotient of 10. Unfortunately, this was all done in the dark. The group does not remember the original Secret Number it divided. Find the original Secret Number. _____

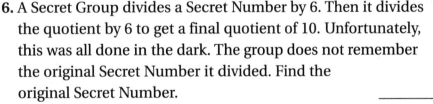

1245 A.D. French King Larry LeDividend scores a huge victory in the Battle of Ratio. What is his secret? He *divides* his army into equal-sized groups. People begin to take notice of this idea. Division is finally on the rise once again.

7. The French army of 147 soldiers needs to cross a river. Each boat can hold 7 soldiers. How many boats does the French army need? _____

Name_____ Date_____

Adventures in Division Part I

Solve these Division Timeline problems.

443 B.C. Dividicus

1. Dividicus took a 37-ounce piece of cheese pie for himself from the 77-ounce pie. How large a piece did each of his 5 friends get if the remaining pie was divided equally? _____

410 B.C. Quo Shun

2. Quo Shun divided a number by 5 and got a remainder of 4. What is the greatest number under 70 that Quo Shun could have divided? _____

195 B.C. Turkish horse tribes

3. The six sub-chiefs needed to divide their 258 horses into 4 groups to give to the sub-sub-chiefs. How many horses did each sub-sub-chief get? Find two ways in which the leftover horses could be divided among the sub-sub-chiefs. _____

62 B.C. The Romans

4. The Roman army could travel 238 miles in 1 week. At this rate, how many miles could they travel in 2 days? (**Hint:** 1 week = 7 days) _____

127 A.D. The Dark Ages

5. Use multiplication to find the quotient of 785 ÷ 4. What is the remainder? What number would you need to add to 785 to get a quotient with no remainder? _____

844 A.D. The Secret Group

6. The Secret Group divides a Secret Number by 9. Then it divides that quotient by 9 to get a final quotient of 12. What is the Secret Number? _____

1245 A.D. French King Larry LeDividend

7. A smaller army of 50 needed to cross a river. Each boat can hold 6 soldiers. How many boats does the army need? How many soldiers will be on the last boat? _____

Mega-Funny Division Stories Scholastic Professional Books

Name_____ Date_____

Adventures in Division

Part II: A Division Timeline

The timeline of division from pages 32–33 continues. (My, how time flies when you're having fun!) As we left page 33, division had been a forgotten skill for hundreds of years. But finally, in the 15th century, division began to make a remarkable comeback . . .

Solve the problems on the timeline.

1453 A.D. The Rebirth of Division. Scientist Leonardo Da Vizzi invents the remainder, the funny-looking bracket thing $\overline{)}$ and ÷, that goofy division symbol.

1. Da Vizzi was also a great painter. He used 135 tubes of paint in 3 months. At this rate, how many tubes would you expect the painter to use in 5 months?   _____

1787 A.D. The writers of the U.S. Constitution use division to divide sandwiches during a meeting.

2. Nine of the writers ordered a huge 144-inch-long Philly cheese steak sandwich at the Founding Fathers Sub Shop. Then Ben Franklin got an upset stomach. Now 8 writers will split the sub. How long would each piece have been when 9 people were going to split the sandwich? How long was each piece when 8 people split the sandwich?   _____

1840 A.D. Pioneers traveling west cross The Great Divide. "Where's the remainder?" many of them are heard to ask.

3. The pioneers traveled 65 miles in 7 days by wagon. At this rate, can they make it to Dodge City, which is 200 miles away, in 1 month? Use estimation to find your answer. (**Hint:** Use 30 days for a month.)   _____

1863 A.D. In a speech, Abraham Lincoln says, "United we stand. Divided we fall." Division goes out of style for several years.

4. In the 1862 election, Lincoln got 64, 106, 47, 85, and 138 votes from 5 different towns near Bear Creek. What was the average number of votes he got? _____

1955 A.D. The calculator is invented. Now everyone can divide like a pro.

5. One thing that calculators don't do well is remainders. The quotient of 620 ÷ 9 is 68.88889. What is this quotient with a remainder? _____

2002 A.D. and beyond . . . In the future, who knows what will happen to division? Will there be another Golden Age? Or will there be another Dark Age in which division will be cast aside and forgotten? Only time will tell.

Name_____ Date_____

Adventures in Division Part II

Solve these Division Timeline problems.

1453 A.D. The Rebirth of Division

1. Da Vizzi sold paintings for 74, 20, 117, and 41 ducats. What was the average price, in ducats, of one of his paintings? _____

1787 A.D. Writers of the U.S. Constitution

2. Five writers split a batch of 99 French fries. The leftover fries were given, one by one, to as many of those writers as possible. How many writers did *not* get an extra fry? _____

1840 A.D. Pioneers

3. Another group of pioneers traveled 55 miles in 6 days. While they traveled, they used 30 pounds of flour a week to make bread. They had 60 pounds of flour. Did their flour last until they reached Cheyenne, which was 100 miles away? Use estimation to find your answer. _____

1863 A.D. Abraham Lincoln Speech

4. In 5 Hampshire County towns, Lincoln averaged exactly 100 votes. The first four votes were 68, 143, 112, and 56. How many votes did Lincoln get in the fifth town? _____

1955 A.D. Invention of Calculator

5. On a calculator, the quotient of 234 ÷ 7 is 33.428571. What is this quotient with a remainder? _____

2002 A.D. and Beyond

6. An unknown dividend was divided by an unknown divisor to get a quotient of 87. If the divisor was less than 10, and the dividend was between 500 and 600, what were the unknown numbers? _____

7. An unknown dividend was divided by an unknown divisor to get a quotient of 43. If the divisor was *even* and less than 10, and the dividend was between 300 and 400, what were the unknown numbers? _____

Name_____ Date_____

Division True or False

Some strange and amazing claims have been made about division. Which claims are true, and which are false? You be the judge. Read each statement, and then write a check in the True or False box.

- **Division has 8 essential vitamins and minerals.**   true ❑   false ❑
- **Remainders are things that hold up a pair of trousers.**   true ❑   false ❑
- **Like snowflakes, no two division problems are alike.**   true ❑   false ❑
- **Division makes a great holiday gift.**   true ❑   false ❑
- **Division is the cause of most traffic jams.**   true ❑   false ❑
- **Division can be used as a delicious barbecue sauce.**   true ❑   false ❑
- **In the Old West, division was against the law.**   true ❑   false ❑
- **While you sleep, your brain computes division problems.**   true ❑   false ❑
- **Sometimes it rains divisors and dividends.**   true ❑   false ❑
- **Some rare division problems are worth millions of dollars.**   true ❑   false ❑
- **Some division problems are as deep as the Grand Canyon.**   true ❑   false ❑
- **Some division problems are poisonous.**   true ❑   false ❑
- **Division helps prevent tooth decay.**   true ❑   false ❑
- **Division appeared in the World Series seven years in a row.**   true ❑   false ❑
- **Using division could prevent most traffic jams.**   true ❑   false ❑
- **Dividing with 2-digit divisors is easy to learn!**   true ❑   false ❑

In fact, only the final statement is true. How do you divide using 2-digit divisors? To solve a problem like 167 ÷ 20, follow the steps on the next page.

1. Write down the problem.
To find out where to write the quotient, go digit by digit until you get a number big enough to divide.

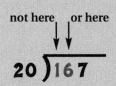

2. Can the first digit, 1, be divided by 20?
No, so don't write anything above the 1. Don't write above the 6 either because 16 cannot be divided by 20.

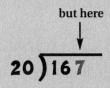

3. Can 167 be divided by 20?
Yes, so write your quotient over the 7.

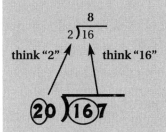

4. Now look at the problem.
Estimate by thinking of 20 as 2 and 167 as 16.
Think: What is 16 divided by 2? The answer is 8.

5. Try 8 as your quotient.
Multiply 20 by 8 to get 160. Subtract to find the remainder. The quotient is 8 with a remainder of 7.

$$
\begin{array}{r}
8\ R\ 7 \\
20\overline{)167} \\
-160 \\
\hline
7
\end{array}
$$

Name_____ Date_____

Division True or False

True or false—it's time for you to solve the following division problems. TRUE!

1. $20\overline{)120}$ 2. $30\overline{)152}$ 3. $40\overline{)206}$ 4. $30\overline{)720}$

5. $50\overline{)456}$ 6. $60\overline{)243}$ 7. $20\overline{)540}$ 8. $40\overline{)864}$

9. $70\overline{)776}$ 10. $60\overline{)982}$ 11. $20\overline{)687}$ 12. $70\overline{)519}$

13. $50\overline{)550}$ 14. $30\overline{)777}$ 15. $80\overline{)294}$ 16. $90\overline{)478}$

17. $60\overline{)373}$ 18. $90\overline{)644}$ 19. $70\overline{)566}$ 20. $40\overline{)870}$

21. The world's fastest divider completed 420 division problems in 20 seconds. On the average, how many problems did he do per second? (**P.S.** He got every problem wrong!)

   _____

22. The world's slowest divider took 50 years to solve 750 division problems. How many problems did she solve each year?

   _____

23. The *S.S. Divisor* is a cruise ship. It traveled 960 miles in 30 days. On average, how many miles did the ship travel each day?

   _____

Mega-Funny Division Stories Scholastic Professional Books

Name_____ Date_____

What Dogs Want: A Survey

What do dogs want?
We asked 100 dogs about their
likes and dislikes.

Here is what we found.

What dogs want:

(1) food

(2) belly rubs

(3) more food

(4) still more food

What dogs don't want:

(1) fleas

(2) lettuce

(3) a laptop computer

(4) dog booties

What dogs like:

(1) bones

(2) naps

(3) walks

(4) something to bark at

What dogs don't like:

(1) cats

(2) mail carriers

(3) napkins

(4) bubble baths

What dogs know:

(1) never trust a cat

(2) bark first, ask questions later

(3) when in doubt, take a nap

What dogs would like to learn:

(1) how to open door knobs

(2) how to open a can of dog food

(3) **how to divide a 3-digit number like 683 by 31.**

Dogs (and people) who would like to know how to find the quotient for a problem like $31\overline{)683}$ should follow the steps on the next page.

1. Write down the problem.

To find out where to write the quotient, go digit by digit until you get a number big enough to divide.

$$31 \overline{)683}$$

2. Can the first digit, 6, be divided by 31?

No, so you should move to the next digit.
Can 68 be divided by 31?
Yes, so write the first digit of the quotient over the 8.

not here   but here

$$31 \overline{)683}$$

3. Use estimation.

Think of 31 as 3 and 68 as 7.
Think: What is 7 divided by 3?
The answer is 2.

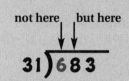

think "3"   think "7"

$$31 \overline{)683}$$

4. Try 2 as your quotient.

Multiply 31 by 2 to get 62. Subtract.

$$
\begin{array}{r}
2 \\
31{\overline{)683}} \\
-62 \\
\hline
6
\end{array}
$$

5. Bring down the 3.

Now divide 68 by 31.
Think: What is 7 divided by 3?
Divide as you normally would until you finish the problem.
The quotient is 22 with a remainder of 1.

$$
\begin{array}{r}
22\ \text{R}1 \\
31{\overline{)683}} \\
-62 \\
\hline
63 \\
-62 \\
\hline
1
\end{array}
$$

Name_____ Date_____

What Dogs Want

Solve these division problems.

1. $21\overline{)126}$

2. $32\overline{)160}$

3. $43\overline{)172}$

4. $24\overline{)192}$

5. $23\overline{)299}$

6. $16\overline{)832}$

7. $37\overline{)962}$

8. $29\overline{)696}$

9. $32\overline{)849}$

10. $13\overline{)728}$

11. $67\overline{)888}$

12. $54\overline{)949}$

13. $31\overline{)1,333}$

14. $24\overline{)1,272}$

15. $36\overline{)2,052}$

16. $46\overline{)3,266}$

17. $73\overline{)4,215}$

18. $59\overline{)6,118}$

19. $66\overline{)8,927}$

20. $94\overline{)4,378}$

21. One person running for governor promised to give free bones to dogs. He'd give each dog 832 bones a year. How many bones per week is this? (**Hint:** There are 52 weeks in a year.)

_____

22. Sniffles has 986 bones. If she buries 58 bones each day, how long will it take her to bury all the bones?

_____

23. Woovis likes to howl for 45 minutes each day. How many *months* will it take Woovis to howl 4,050 minutes? (**Hint:** Use 30 days for a month.)

_____

Name_____ Date_____

Election 2004: What the Voters Care About Most

The results are in for this year's election.

Listed below are the things that voters care about most.

Question: What's the biggest problem facing our nation at this point in time?

A. Those annoying ketchup packets that are hard to open

B. Being invaded by gigantic hideous spider monsters from outer space

C. Really ugly shoes

Solve these big problems.

Problem 1: Each annoying ketchup packet holds 24 grams of ketchup. A big bottle of ketchup holds 744 grams of ketchup. How many annoying packets would it take to fill a big bottle of ketchup?   _____

Problem 2: A hideous spider monster can shoot 44 ounces of horrible black ink at its enemies at one time. The spider monster has a 792-ounce supply of ink. How many extra squirts will the spider monster get if it shot 36-ounce squirts instead of 44-ounce squirts?   _____

Problem 3: Last year 1 out of every 18 people in the town of Mayberry were stricken with ugly shoes. This year, 1 out of every 15 people had ugly shoes. If Mayberry has 540 people, how many more people had ugly shoes this year?   _____

Question: What important problems do we face in the future?

A. Ballpoint pens may run out of ink.

B. Our hair could become dry and lifeless.

C. Hideous spider monsters from outer space could take over
our government.

Problem 4: A ballpoint pen can write a single line that is
4,000 feet long before it runs out of ink. If your full signature
were 12 inches long, how many signatures could you write
with a single pen? (**Hint:** 1 foot has 12 inches.) _____

Problem 5: Larry's hair grew 570 mm in 19 months. On average,
how long did his hair grow each month? _____

Problem 6: In an election for mayor, former mayor Joe Smith
received 27,269 votes. The Hideous Spider Monster got
32,573 votes. There were 52 districts in the city. On average,
how many more votes did the Hideous Spider Monster receive
in each district? _____

Name_____ Date_____

Election 2004: What the Voters Care About Most

Solve these problems.

Question: How do you think we can best solve the problems of the future?

A. Everyone should work together.

B. Everyone should work separately.

C. No one should work at all.

D. Gigantic, hideous spider monsters from outer space should solve our problems.

1. Suppose we have 756 problems to solve. If 18 people work together to solve the problems, how many problems would each person need to solve? _____

2. Suppose 4 of the 18 people from the problem above don't solve any problems at all. How many problems would each of the remaining people need to solve? _____

3. Suppose all 756 problems are divided equally among the 18 people. What if 8 of the 18 people solve only half as many problems as they should have solved? How many problems would each of the remaining people need to solve? How many problems would be leftover? _____

4. A single hideous spider monster can solve 3 times as many problems as a person. How many spider monsters would it take to replace all of the 18 people who are solving the 756 problems? How many problems would each spider monster solve? _____

Mega-Funny Division Stories Scholastic Professional Books

Name_____ Date_____

Are We Running Out of Jokes?

The National Humor Council has issued a serious warning: America is running out of jokes! The situation is very serious. The council estimates that the Strategic Joke Reserve (number of jokes saved up) is at its lowest point since the 1950s!

102,342 jokes

JOKES
SAVED
UP

32,056 jokes

25,913 jokes

**Jokes Used
(each year)**

**New Jokes Created
(each year)**

Strategic Joke Reserve

Use ESTIMATION to solve the problems.

1. About how many jokes are created each year? About how many jokes are used up? What is the loss or gain of jokes?   _____

2. At the current rate, about how many years do we have until we completely use up the Strategic Joke Reserve (SJR)?   _____

3. About how many years would our Strategic Joke Reserve (SJR) last if we used jokes at our normal rate and no new jokes were created at all?   _____

What Can Be Done?

Smirk Smedly, America's Secretary of Humor, says there are three ways to protect America's Humor Supply.

- **Conserve and recycle jokes.**
- **Explore new joke ideas, including laughing at things that aren't really funny.**
- **Attack the root of the problem—laughter.**

Recycling: Recycled jokes can get boring. Recently a performer at a comedy club repeated the same stale joke over and over again for an entire hour! While we applaud his efforts at saving humor, we recognize that there are limits to recycling.

Laughing at Un-Funny Things: It's easier than you think. Laugh at a chair. Laugh at a weather report. Laugh at a roll of tape! These activities may sound silly, but they SAVE jokes!

Stop Laughing: The Secretary of Humor says we could save 8,106 jokes each year if we just stopped laughing.

The Future

Recent discoveries in the Arctic wilderness have discovered a VAST supply of jokes, cracks, puns, quips, and jests. Some experts estimate that these funny things could keep us chuckling for a HUNDRED years.

What YOU Can Do

DON'T LAUGH. When someone says something funny, just sit there. Don't laugh. TEACH YOUR CHILDREN. If they have to smile or laugh, they should cover their mouths so the laughter doesn't spread. Keep in mind that every joke we chuckle at today leaves one less yuck for our grandchildren and great-grandchildren.

Name_____ Date_____

Are We Running Out of Jokes?

Use estimation to solve these problems.

102,342 jokes

JOKES SAVED UP

32,056 jokes

25,913 jokes

**Jokes Used
(each year)**

**New Jokes Created
(each year)**

Strategic Joke Reserve

1. The Humor Council estimates that we can save 951 jokes a year through recycling. If this occurs, will the Strategic Joke Reserve (SJR) get larger or smaller? Explain.

_____

2. How would recycling jokes and saving 2,149 jokes change the number of years that the SJR would last?

_____

3. Suppose laughing at un-funny things could save 4,735 jokes a year. How would this affect the SJR? Would it shrink or grow? Explain.

_____

4. How would laughing at un-funny things to save 4,735 jokes change the number of years that the SJR would last?

_____

5. If everyone stopped laughing, what would happen to the SJR? Would it shrink or grow? Explain.

_____

6. If 8,106 jokes a year were saved by not laughing, about how many years would it take to double the size of the SJR?

_____

Name_____ Date_____

Mental Man: He Can Read Your Mind!

Today's Episode:
Trouble at Café ESP

I, Mental Man, was sitting at Café ESP, reading the newspaper. The trouble was, it wasn't my own newspaper.

"Stop staring at me or I'll call the police!" the man at the next table said to me.

"Don't be alarmed," I chuckled. "I'm not staring at you. I'm Mental Man. I was just reading your mind as you read your paper!"

To show my AMAZING mental powers I did these Mental Math tricks.

First, I demonstrated how to divide by 10. Fill in the missing numbers.

$30 \div 10 = 3$ $80 \div 10 = $ _____

$40 \div 10 = 4$ $100 \div 10 = $ _____

$50 \div 10 = 5$ $120 \div 10 = $ _____

$60 \div 10 = 6$ $150 \div 10 = $ _____

$70 \div 10 = 7$ $270 \div 10 = $ _____

"I don't care about your Mental Math tricks," said the man. "I'm still calling the police."

"Wait," I said. "Check out these Mental Math techniques."

Use mental math to fill in the blanks.

$6 \div 2 = 3$ $15 \div 3 = 5$ $24 \div 4 = 6$

$60 \div 20 = 3$ $150 \div 30 = 5$ $240 \div 40 = $ _____

$600 \div 20 = $ _____ $1,500 \div 30 = $ _____ $2,400 \div 40 = $ _____

$6,000 \div 20 = $ _____ $15,000 \div 30 = $ _____ $24,000 \div 40 = $ _____

"What seems to be the problem here?" asked the police officer.

"This person is staring at me," said the man.

"No, I'm not," I said. "I'm Mental Man. I was just mentally reading his newspaper—and performing some mental math tricks. Would you like to see some?"

Before the officer could answer, I read his mind. "You're impressed with my Mental Math tricks and you're going to let me go," I said.

"Not quite," said the policeman. "I'm going to haul you in for breaking Code 423-A—Illegal Mind-Reading."

So that's how I, Mental Man, was arrested. But don't worry. While I was at the police station I amused myself by doing mental math. I solved these problems.

Can you solve these problems yourself?

$270 \div 30 =$ _____

$2{,}700 \div 300 =$ _____

$27{,}000 \div 300 =$ _____

Name_____ Date_____

Mental Man: He Can Read Your Mind!

Use mental math to solve these problems.

1. $25 \div 5 = 5$

$250 \div 50 =$ _____

$2,500 \div 500 =$ _____

$25,000 \div 500 =$ _____

2. $18 \div 6 = 3$

$180 \div 60 =$ _____

$1,800 \div 600 =$ _____

$18,000 \div 600 =$ _____

3. $24 \div 4 = 6$

$240 \div 40 =$ _____

$2,400 \div 400 =$ _____

$24,000 \div 400 =$ _____

4. $350 \div 50 =$ _____

$3,500 \div 500 =$ _____

$35,000 \div 500 =$ _____

5. $360 \div 60 =$ _____

$3,600 \div 600 =$ _____

$36,000 \div 600 =$ _____

6. $450 \div 90 =$ _____

$4,500 \div 900 =$ _____

$45,000 \div 900 =$ _____

7. Write a rule to describe how to divide by 10 using mental math.

_____

_____

_____

8. Write a rule for dividing by numbers that end in zero.

_____

_____

_____

Mega-Funny Division Stories Scholastic Professional Books

Name_____ Date_____

Martha Bussell Selects the Best Numbers for You!

Hello, I'm Martha Bussell. Are numbers special to you? They are to me.
If you have a question about a number, write to me, Martha Bussell. And remember to use my Martha Bussell Divisibility Rules no matter which number you choose.

Martha Bussell's Divisibility Rules

2s: All even numbers are divisible by 2.

3s: If the sum of the digits is divisible by 3, the number is divisible by 3.

4s: If the last 2 digits are divisible by 4, the number is divisible by 4.

5s: If the last digit is 0 or 5, the number is divisible by 5.

6s: If the number is even and divisible by 3, the number is divisible by 6.

9s: If the sum of the digits is divisible by 9, the number is divisible by 9.

10s: If the last digit is 0, the number is divisible by 10.

Dear Martha,

I'd like to get my boyfriend a special number for his birthday. He likes numbers that are divisible by 2. I'm thinking of something between 73 and 83. Can you think of a good number to give him?

Signed, Wants to Get Boyfriend a Good Number

Dear Wants,

Your boyfriend sounds like a very EVEN fellow. How about giving him the number 74? It's the perfect number for someone with his *even* interests.

Signed, Martha

Can you think of two other numbers to give to the boyfriend?

_____

*Which number can she give to her boyfriend that is divisible by 3
as well as 2?*

_____

Dear Martha,

On the soccer team, I wear the uniform with the number 55 on it. I love 55, but I
need to change to a 3-digit number that is divisible by 3 and has 55 as its last two
digits. Can you think of something?

Signed, Number 55

Dear Number 55,

I've always found the number 255 to be UTTERLY CHARMING! Why don't you try
that? It has everything you need in a number—and more.

Good luck, Martha

Which number besides 255 could Number 55 use?

_____

What is the highest 3-digit number that Number 55 could use?

_____

That's all the letters about numbers for today!

Name_____ Date_____

Martha Bussell Selects the Best Numbers for You!

Read the letters to Martha, and then write your own answers to them.

Dear Martha,

At the beach last summer, I got this great 3-digit number. All 3 digits were the same. It was divisible by both 4 and 3. Then I forgot what the number was. Can you think of it?

Signed, Beach Bunny

Think about which number Bunny could use.

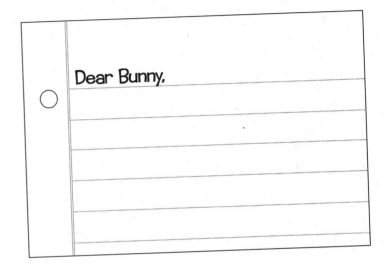

1. Can you think of a second 3-digit number (with all the same digits) for Bunny?

_____

Dear Martha,

The only numbers I'm really attracted to are divisible by 10, 9, 6, 5, 3, and 2. Can you think of a 3-digit number for me?

Signed, Picky

Think of a number that Picky would like.

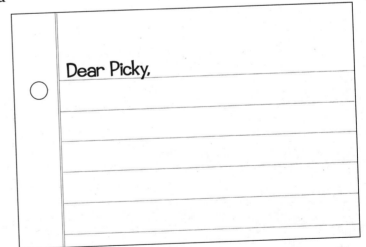

2. Can you think of a second number for Picky?

_____

Name_____ Date_____

Future Gum

Amazing New Gum Will Solve All Your Problems!

While the gum of the past was just something to chew, future gum will be much more than that. Check out these fabulous new gums that are coming soon to gum stores near you.

INTELLI-GUM: The World's Most Intelligent gum
• It has 512 Mega-Bites of Giga-GUM memory.
• It can do your homework for you.
• It can balance your checkbook, solve crossword puzzles, and much more.
• It does all the work—while you sit back and chew.
• It comes in 3 great flavors—Genius Grape, Crafty Chocolate, and Egg-Head Orange.

Solve the problem by turning the fraction into division. Use the denominator as the divisor.

Intelli-Gum comes in a pack of 30 sticks of gum. Suppose you chewed $\frac{1}{2}$ the pack. How many pieces would you chew in all?

numerator ⟶ $\frac{1}{2}$ of **30** ⟶ $2\overline{)30}^{\,15}$
denominator ⟶

Suppose you chewed $\frac{1}{4}$ of a 200-pack. How many pieces would you chew?

$\frac{1}{4}$ of **200** ⟶ $4\overline{)200}^{\,50}$

Suppose you chewed $\frac{1}{5}$ of a 40-pack. How many pieces would you chew?

$\frac{1}{5}$ of **40** _____

SHY-GUY-GUM: The Gum for Shy People
• You chew. It makes friends.
• This gum is great for parties.
• Use Shy-Guy Gum to meet people everywhere—in buses, crowded elevators, or shopping lines.
• It comes in 4 terrific flavors—Outgoing Orange, Vivacious Vanilla, Sociable Strawberry, and Howdy There Chocolate.

Shy-Guy-Gum comes in a pack of 30 sticks. Two-thirds of the pack is Vivacious Vanilla. How much is this?

First find $\frac{1}{3}$ of 30.

$$\frac{1}{3} \text{ of } 30 \longrightarrow 3\overline{)30}^{\,10}$$

Then multiply $\frac{1}{3}$ (the quotient) by 2 to get $\frac{2}{3}$.   2 x 10 = **20**

Lucy chewed 36 sticks of Shy-Guy-Gum. Of the sticks she chewed, $\frac{3}{4}$ were Howdy There Chocolate. How many sticks of Howdy There Chocolate did Lucy chew?

First find $\frac{1}{4}$ of 36.

$$\frac{1}{4} \text{ of } 36 \longrightarrow 4\overline{)36}^{\,9}$$

Then multiply the quotient by 3.   3 x 9 = **27**

Remember, always buy your gum from a licensed gum professional.

Name_____ Date_____

Future Gum

Read about the latest gum, and then solve the problems.

GABBY-GUM: The World's Only Talking Gum
• You chew. It talks.
• It tells you, "I'm running out of flavor."
• It says, "Please dispose of me properly."
• It reminds you, "Please chew responsibly."
• It comes in 4 fabulous flavors—Chattering Cherry, Blabbering Blueberry, Loquacious Lemon, and Shouting Strawberry.

1. A store sold 240 packs of Gabby-Gum. Chattering Cherry made up $\frac{1}{4}$ of the sales. How many packs of Chattering Cherry were sold? _____

2. In a different store, $\frac{1}{6}$ of 144 packs of Gabby-Gum were Blabbering Blueberry. How many packs was this? _____

Now solve the following problems.

3. $\frac{1}{3}$ of 24 = _____   4. $\frac{1}{4}$ of 60 = _____   5. $\frac{1}{5}$ of 100 = _____

6. $\frac{1}{2}$ of 120 = _____   7. $\frac{1}{6}$ of 120 = _____   8. $\frac{1}{8}$ of 160 = _____

9. $\frac{1}{9}$ of 144 = _____   10. $\frac{1}{7}$ of 252 = _____   11. $\frac{1}{9}$ of 99 = _____

12. $\frac{1}{8}$ of 192 = _____   13. $\frac{1}{10}$ of 260 = _____   14. $\frac{1}{7}$ of 161 = _____

15. $\frac{1}{12}$ of 156 = _____   16. $\frac{1}{20}$ of 500 = _____   17. $\frac{1}{15}$ of 450 = _____

18. $\frac{1}{40}$ of 520 = _____   19. $\frac{2}{3}$ of 24 = _____   20. $\frac{3}{4}$ of 48 = _____

21. $\frac{2}{5}$ of 40 = _____   22. $\frac{5}{6}$ of 30 = _____   23. $\frac{3}{8}$ of 96 = _____

24. $\frac{3}{5}$ of 150 = _____   25. $\frac{5}{9}$ of 180 = _____   26. $\frac{3}{10}$ of 440 = _____

Name_____ Date_____

The National Soil Association presents:

DIRT: It's Better Than Ever!

As a child, you loved it. You played in it.
And then, somehow you became convinced that dirt was BAD!
But it isn't! Just read these words of support.

Rock Gimlet, Movie Star:

I love dirt. I use it in all my movies.
It's great for the ground, for the
backyard, and even for flowerbeds.
For my birthday, my wife bought
me a 47.2-pound Bucket 'O Dirt.
I divided it into 8 different bags.
How many pounds did each bag
contain?

**Here's how to divide decimals
by whole numbers.**

Bring up the decimal point.

$$8\overline{)47.2}$$

Then divide as you would
normally.

$$
\begin{array}{r}
5.9 \\
8\overline{)47.2} \\
-40 \\
\hline
72 \\
72 \\
\hline
0
\end{array}
$$

Divide by whole numbers to solve the following problems.

Tanya Wiggle-White, Pro Soccer Player: Our soccer field is made of dirt. Without dirt, I would never have scored the winning goal in the Big Game. And I never would have appeared on the front of the Wuggies breakfast cereal box. I owe everything to dirt. If I divide a 28.2-ounce box of Wuggies into 6 bowls, how many ounces will each bowl contain?

_____

Baba Hum Drum, Musician: For a long time, I wasn't into dirt. Then one day I was riding through a cornfield. I thought, "Wow, look at all that dirt." I wrote a song about it called "Wow, Look at All That Dirt." I made 4.8 million dollars with that song in 8 months. On average, how many millions did I make each month?

_____

Chuck Bunsen, Guy Who Talks on the Phone: Hey, as a guy who talks on the phone a lot, you wouldn't think I'd be a big fan of dirt, but I am. Why? Because it is what it is. It doesn't drive a fancy car. It doesn't wear cool clothes or expensive jewelry. It's just dirt. It just sits there. I paid $58.40 for 8 tons of Ordinary Dirt. How much did each ton cost?

_____

Roscoe Folger, Dirt Scientist: Did you know the following dirty facts?
• Dirt has no artificial colorings or flavorings.
• Ancient people built large structures with dirt called "Big Piles of Dirt."
• Mud is made from dirt and water.
• Pound for pound, dirt is the dirtiest substance on Earth.
• Dirt can be used as fuel for your car if you run out of gasoline.[1]

Suppose you drove 324.8 miles on 20 gallons of gas. [2]
How many miles can you drive on one gallon?

_____

[1] After adding dirt, most cars will stall after 1.4 seconds and not re-start. Your actual results may vary.

[2] Before you put the dirt in the car and it stalled

Name_____ Date_____

DiRT

Read these words of support for dirt. Then solve each division problem.

Fran-Swah LeVoo, Gourmet Cook: Where I come from, we make a delicious dish called Dirt Stew. Take 5.24 kg of dirt. Add 4.64 kg of sticks and stones. Now cook for 14 hours or until the mixture turns an ugly mud color. Divide the mixture into 13 bowls. How many kilograms will each bowl contain? Once bowls are divided, pour the mixture down the sink. Now make yourself a sandwich and eat it. Your sandwich will taste much better than this terrible dish.

_____

Bobo Fletcher, Dirt-Ball Maker: You can make Little Dirt Balls or Big Ones. For Little Dirt Balls, take 76.32 ounces of dirt. Divide it into 24 equal-sized portions. How much will each portion weigh? For Big Ones take the same 76.32 ounces and divide it into 9 portions. How much will each portion weigh? Dirt balls make great gifts. You can also take them and drop them in the river.

_____

Now solve these problems.

1. $4.8 \div 2 =$ _____

2. $2.5 \div 5 =$ _____

3. $2.44 \div 4 =$ _____

4. $7.2 \div 6 =$ _____

5. $37.6 \div 8 =$ _____

6. $7.29 \div 3 =$ _____

7. $42.42 \div 7 =$ _____

8. $571.05 \div 9 =$ _____

9. $43.2 \div 16 =$ _____

10. $60.2 \div 43 =$ _____

11. $109.5 \div 25 =$ _____

12. $781.26 \div 58 =$ _____

Name_____ Date_____

The Annoying Dragon

Life was good in the far-off kingdom of King Larry until the dragon came. The dragon would scare people with his roar, melt things with his fire-breath, and bore people with his endless chatter about numbers. It was getting to be a problem, so King Larry issued a proclamation. Any hero who could defeat the Annoying Dragon would be granted any wish by the king.

Dozens of heroes came. They had strong muscles, powerful swords, and mighty horses. But the dragon easily defeated them. First he used his fiery breath to melt their swords. Then he forced them to solve difficult math problems.

"Hey, this isn't fair!" the heroes whined.

"Can't somebody do something?" asked King Larry.

Finally, a young girl named Molly came forward. "I can defeat the dragon."

The heroes of the court were outraged. "She's no hero!" they cried. "She's just a young girl! If she succeeds, it will make the rest of us look like fools."

"You're right," said King Larry. "We can't allow our best heroes to look foolish. I'm sorry, young lady. If you want to defeat this dragon, you'll need to do it on your own."

That's exactly what Molly did. She went to the Enchanted Forest. She saw the dragon.

"Solve this problem: Divide 2.62 by 0.04," commanded the dragon.

Molly solved it! Look at the next page to see how she did it.

The dragon was astonished, but he still wasn't satisfied. He gave her more problems. Some of these problems were quite tricky, but Molly was brave. She solved all the problems.

When Molly completed the problems, she went back to King Larry and told him she'd defeated the dragon.

"That's impossible!" cried all of the heroes.

At that point, the Annoying Dragon burst into the room and explained everything. The king saw the error of his ways. He declared that he'd been wrong and granted Molly any wish she liked. Molly wished that the king would organize a Big Division Festival and invite everyone— including the dragon!

King Larry did this, and all went well. The Big Division Festival was a success. Molly was a hero. And the dragon turned out to be quite friendly, once people got to know him— not so boring or annoying after all, for a dragon, anyway.

THE END

Divide: 2.62 ÷ 0.04.

Move the decimal point in the divisor all the way to the right.

$$0.04.\overline{)2.62}$$

Move the decimal point in the dividend the same number of spaces. Write the decimal point in the quotient.

directly above

$$0.04.\overline{)2.62.}$$

Divide as you would normally. Add zeroes if you need them.

$$
\begin{array}{r}
65.5 \\
004.\overline{)262.0} \\
-24 \\
\hline
22 \\
-20 \\
\hline
20 \\
-20 \\
\hline
0
\end{array}
$$

extra zero

Name_____ Date_____

The Annoying Dragon

Use Molly's method to solve these problems yourself.

1. $0.4 \overline{)32.8}$

2. $0.03 \overline{)18.9}$

3. $0.6 \overline{)34.98}$

4. $0.07 \overline{)62.3}$

5. $1.5 \overline{)60.45}$

6. $2.3 \overline{)48.3}$

7. $4.2 \overline{)144.06}$

8. $6.6 \overline{)435.6}$

9. $2.1 \overline{)16.8}$

10. $0.07 \overline{)39.34}$

11. $3.2 \overline{)51.2}$

12. $2.4 \overline{)12.72}$

13. $3.2 \overline{)163.84}$

14. $0.9 \overline{)56.52}$

15. $0.022 \overline{)8.866}$

16. $0.42 \overline{)2.604}$

17. $0.46 \overline{)32.844}$

18. $2.8 \overline{)96.04}$

19. $0.03 \overline{)1.95}$

20. $0.35 \overline{)19.11}$

21. $0.018 \overline{)9.54}$

22. $0.14 \overline{)6.72}$

23. $0.62 \overline{)11.78}$

24. $0.73 \overline{)143.08}$

Mega-Funny Division Stories Scholastic Professional Books

Name_____ Date_____

Martha Bussell's Mathematical Household Hints

Today's Topic: Leftover Remainders

Hello, this is Martha Bussell with another episode of Mathematical Household Hints. Today we're going to talk about REMAINDERS. If you're like me, you love to divide. But what do you do with those MESSY remainders you're left with afterwards? Here are some ideas from my readers.

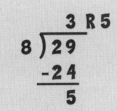

Dear Martha,

When I divide, I like to write the remainder with an R like the problem shown. Is this too old-fashioned?

Signed, No Geezer

$$8 \overline{)29} \quad \begin{array}{r} 3\ R5 \\ \hline -24 \\ \hline 5 \end{array}$$

Dear Martha,

When I divide, I like to express the remainder as a fraction. Does this make sense to you?

Signed, Fractional Fran

$$8 \overline{)29} \quad \begin{array}{r} 3\frac{5}{8} \\ \hline -24 \\ \hline 5 \end{array}$$

Dear Martha,

I'm a person who doesn't know when to stop. So when I divide, I keep going until the decimal stops or I round off. Is this weird?

Signed, Decimal Dave

$$8 \overline{)29.000} \quad \begin{array}{r} 3.625 \\ \hline -24 \\ \hline 50 \\ -48 \\ \hline 20 \\ -16 \\ \hline 40 \\ -40 \end{array}$$

Dear Readers,

In fact, you're ALL correct. You can express a remainder as a WHOLE NUMBER, a FRACTION, or a DECIMAL. Each one works for different situations.

Signed, Martha

Name_____ Date_____

Martha Bussell's Mathematical Household Hints

Martha Bussell has more division problems for you to solve.

1. My book, *Martha Bussell Knows Everything,* has exactly 300 pages and is divided into 7 equal chapters. How many pages are left-over for the index of my book? Explain what remainder method you used and why it works for this problem.

_____

_____

2. I sell my "Martha Bussell Red Ribbons" at my Martha Bussell Mega-Store. Suppose I wanted to cut a 36-inch red ribbon into 15 pieces. How long would each piece be? Explain what remainder method you used and why it works for this problem.

_____

_____

3. At my Mega Store, I also sell "Martha Bussell Whipped Air" in a 5.85-ounce can. Each can has 13 servings. How much does each serving weigh? Explain what remainder method you used and why it works for this problem.

_____

_____

4. My 40-minute TV Special "Martha Bussell Knows More Than You" has 15 commercial breaks. If I divide the breaks up evenly, how far apart will they be in time? Explain what remainder method you used and why it works for this problem.

_____

_____

5. My "Martha Bussell Celebrity Limo Service" fits 16 celebrities into one limo. How many limos will be needed to take 50 celebrities to my fabulous new Martha Bussell Goor-May Restaurant? Explain what remainder method you used and why it works for this problem.

_____

_____

6. Martha Bussell Sports Drink comes in a 64.3-ounce bottle. If I give an equal amount of the drink to all 5 of my personal trainers, how many ounces will each trainer receive? Explain what remainder method you used and why it works for this problem.

_____

_____

7. At my Martha Fitness Center you can have a 20-minute workout for $32. At this rate, how much does each minute of workout time cost? Explain what remainder method you used and why it works for this problem.

_____

_____

8. The $832.50 check at my Martha Bussell Goor-May Restaurant was split evenly among 18 celebrities. How much did each celebrity pay? Explain what remainder method you used and why it works for this problem.

_____

_____

Mega-Funny Division Stories Scholastic Professional Books

Name_____ Date_____

Whopper–The Magazine of Fibs, Falsehoods, Exaggerations, Lies, and Outright Bunk!

Welcome to Whopper!

Each of the 42,000 pages in this issue is jammed with fascinating articles that are 100 percent true and written by award-winning authors.[1]

[1] This is a lie. The articles are not true or fascinating. None of the authors ever won a single award. In fact, this issue really contains only 8.2 pages and was written entirely by Lester Zetch, who has no writing talent whatsoever. There are 902 lies or falsehoods on these 8.2 pages. On average, how many lies or falsehoods per page are there?

_____

Like to read?

Annie Zetch, of Norwood, Ohio, claims she read a 1,626-page book in 5.4 seconds. "It was really interesting," Annie said. "I think."[2]

[2] This is false. The book only had 126 pages. And Annie read it in 12.6 hours. How many pages did Annie actually read each hour? _____

Like to fish?

Bob Zetch, of Norwood, Ohio, claims he caught a 445.3-inch long bass in his own bathtub! Now that's some great fishing![3]

[3] Bob Zetch never caught any fish. He bought the fish at a pet store. And the real fish was only 7.3 inches in length. How many times bigger was the exaggerated fish than the real fish? _____

Mildred Zetch

of Norwood, Ohio, claims that her dog Sniffy works at the post office and makes a salary of $85,000 a week.[4]

[4] This is untrue. Sniffy doesn't work at the post office. He was fired from his job. And if he did work there, Sniffy would make $562.10 for 38.5 hours of work. How much money is this per hour? _____

Name_____ Date_____

Whopper

Solve these division problems—without using fibs, falsehoods, exaggerations, lies, or outright bunk!

Jackie Zetch of Norwood, Ohio, says she drove 162,000 miles on 6.4 gallons of gas! [1]

[1] This is nonsense. Jackie Zetch doesn't own a car. And she doesn't know how to drive. If she did, she would drive 147.2 miles on 6.4 gallons of gas. How many miles per gallon is this?

_____

Marty Zetch of Norwood, Ohio, claims that his hair has appeared as a guest star on TV over 368 times. "I have the most popular hair in Hollywood," Marty says. [2]

[2] This is a fib. Marty's hair has never been on TV. Marty *has* watched TV, however. He watched 15.75 hours of TV in 6.3 days. How many hours of TV did he watch each day, on average?

_____

Lisa Zetch of Norwood, Ohio, told 8,234 lies in 4.7 seconds. This was the fastest lying that has ever been done. [3]

[3] This is a lie. Lisa told only 1,320 lies in 16.5 minutes. On average, how many lies per minute was this?

_____

Sasha Zetch of Norwood, Ohio, taught a squirrel named Kikkie how to play 242,000 songs on the piano in only one week.[4]

[4] This is untrue. The squirrel does not play the piano. But it did bury 1,196 nuts in 18.4 days. On average, how many nuts did it bury each day?

_____

Name_____ Date_____

Great Achievement / Bad Hair

Great moments in history— from a "hair" point of view!

What role did hair play in history? Find out by solving these problems.

Washington Crosses the Delaware:

George Washington's heroic crossing of the icy Delaware River in December of 1778 is a moment that will live on in history. Was Washington having a Bad Hair Day during this historic moment?

1. "He never had enough time for a decent haircut," said Freddy Dobbs, Washington's barber. In 1778, Washington paid a total $2.70 for a total of 7 shaves and haircuts. He got one more shave than haircut. How many of each did he get? _____

Ye Olde Barber Shoppe
Haircut 42 cents
Shave 36 cents

2. "I never liked his hair style," said Martha Washington, George's wife. "It was too long and droopy. He looked like a sheep." Washington's hair grew 3.2 inches in 5 months. At this rate, how many inches would it grow in an entire year? _____

Barbara McClintock Discovers "Jumping Genes": Famous scientist Barbara McClintock won the Nobel Prize for discovering "jumping genes." Was McClintock having a Bad Hair Day on the day she made her big discovery?

3. "Barbara had a bad hair day whenever she went swimming and worked in a cold room on the same day," said lab assistant Tommy Lee. Barbara went swimming every 15 days. She worked in the cold room every 20 days. Suppose Barbara went swimming and worked in the cold room on the first of the month and had a bad hair day. When would you expect her to have her next bad hair day? _____

Name_____ Date_____

Great Achievement / Bad Hair

Solve these hair-raising problems.

1. Refer to page 69. Starting on January 1 with a bad hair day, how many bad hair days would you expect Barbara McClintock to have in a year?

_____

2. For problem 1, during what months of the year would Barbara have bad hair days? What months would have no bad hair days?

_____

Napoleon is Defeated at Waterloo. After a string of brilliant victories, Napoleon Bonaparte finally was defeated by the British at the battle of Waterloo in 1803. Did bad hair have something to do with the defeat of Napoleon's army?

3. Each soldier in Napoleon's army used 0.8 ounces of hair gel per day. A giant vat held 3,000 ounces of gel. It was filled up for the soldiers every day. How many soldiers were in Napoleon's army?

_____

4. Hair historians estimate that each of Napoleon's divisions had only 240 quarts of hair gel for 2,400 soldiers. If each soldier used 0.8 ounce of gel per day, how many days' supply did the troops have? (**Hint:** One quart has 32 ounces.)

_____

5. Napoleon suggested that each soldier cut back to 0.5 ounces of hair gel per day. How many days' supply would the 2,400 soldiers now have?

_____

6. Napoleon himself used 1.6 ounces of hair gel each day. If his troops did the same thing, how many days' supply would they have?

_____

Chuck the Friendly. p. 9: **1.** 2 pigs in each group   **2.** 4 pigs in each group
3. 3 crowns in each group   **4.** 2 crowns in each group   **5.** 4 apples in each group
6. 2 apples in each group   **7.** Answers will vary.

Suzy Sawyer. pp. 10-11: **1.** 3 logs   **2.** 4 logs   **3.** 6 logs   **4.** 2 logs   **5.** 4 oz   **6.** 5 oz
7. 4 oz   **8.** 3
p. 12: **1.** 6 yds   **2.** 3 yds   **3.** 9   **4.** 2   **5.** Answers will vary.

Divisor, Quotient, Dividend. p. 14: **1.** 2   **2.** 15   **3.** 3   **4.** 4   **5.** divisor   **6.** dividend   **7.** 6
8. dividend   **9.** 12   **10.** 7   **11.** 5   **12.** 8   **13.** dividend   **14.** 25 + 6 = 31

Professor Kingsley. p. 16: **1.** 3   **2.** 3   **3.** 2   **4.** 9   **5.** 5   **6.** 8   **7.** 5   **8.** 7   **9.** 6 x 3, 3
10. 6 x 4, 4   **11.** 12 ÷ 4 = 3, 12 ÷ 3 = 4   **12.** If you multiply the circled numbers—
the divisor and the quotient—you will get the dividend.

Division Believe It or Not!. p. 17: 5, 4, 2, 6, 3, 5, 2, 8;   4, 2, 5, 3, 5, 3, 6, 2
p. 18: **1.** 7   **2.** 3   **3.** 9   **4.** 8   **5.** 4   **6.** 7   **7.** 9   **8.** 6   **9.** 7   **10.** 8   **11.** 6   **12.** 9   **13.** 8
14. 4   **15.** 7   **16.** 9

The Five Things Millionaires Do. p. 19: 3, 5, 3, 2, 2, 3, 2, 4
p. 20: **1.** 7   **2.** 6   **3.** 9   **4.** 8   **5.** 4   **6.** 9   **7.** 8   **8.** 7   **9.** 6   **10.** 7   **11.** 9   **12.** 8   **13.** 6   **14.** 8
15. 7   **16.** 9   **17.** 2   **18.** 4   **19.** 5   **20.** 6   **21.** 5   **22.** 4   **23.** 3   **24.** 5

Nancy Nimms, Bargain Hunter. pp. 21-22: $4, $3, $2;   **1.** 8   **2.** 1   **3.** 9   **4.** 10; $40,
$30, $20;   **5.** 60   **6.** 90   **7.** 57   **8.** 11; $4, $3, $2;   **9.** 6   **10.** 20   **11.** 30   **12.** 8
p. 23: **1.** 7   **2.** 15   **3.** 23   **4.** 70   **5.** 89   **6.** 6   **7.** 10   **8.** 80   **9.** 7   **10.** 40   **11.** 9   **12.** 60
13. Remove 1 zero from dividend to get quotient.   **14.** Remove 2 zeros from dividend to
get quotient.   **15.** Remove 3 zeros from dividend to get quotient. Possible examples:
9,000 ÷ 1,000 = 9; 80,000 ÷ 1,000 = 80.

Johnnie Diviso. p. 26: **1.** 10   **2.** 11   **3.** 16   **4.** 5   **5.** 10   **6.** 7   **7.** 21   **8.** 21   **9.** 46   **10.** 12
11. 13   **12.** 19   **13.** 24   **14.** 33   **15.** 14   **16.** 12   **17.** 17 cases   **18.** 16 cases
19. 32 lbs, 16 lbs   **20.** 4 hrs

Pierre LeDoo. p. 28: **1.** 11 R1   **2.** 9 R2   **3.** 16 R2   **4.** 10 R4   **5.** 12 R1   **6.** 12 R2   **7.** 14 R2
8. 12 R4   **9.** 11 R2   **10.** 11 R7   **11.** 24 R3   **12.** 25 R2   **13.** 19 R1   **14.** 14 R5   **15.** 12 R4
16. 12 R1   **17.** 14 yd apart, 3 yd   **18.** 12 km, 4 km   **19.** 4 ft   **20.** 2 ft

Cats and Division. p. 31: **1.** 33   **2.** 56   **3.** 72   **4.** 48   **5.** 56   **6.** 93   **7.** 32   **8.** 96   **9.** 213
10. 114   **11.** 69   **12.** 259   **13.** 34   **14.** 98   **15.** 64   **16.** 48   **17.** 34 cats   **18.** 42 days
19. 16 seconds   **20.** 52 walks, 8 walks

Part 1, A Division Timeline. pp. 32-33: **1.** 11 oz   **2.** 34   **3.** 43 horses
4. 8 groups of 97 soldiers, 1 group of 96 soldiers   **5.** 8 x 6 = 48; 55 – 48 = 7; 8 x 9 = 72;
76 – 72 = 4; 69 R4   **6.** 360   **7.** 21 boats
p. 34: **1.** 8 oz   **2.** 69   **3.** 64 R2; answers will vary   **4.** 68 miles   **5.** 196 R1; 3   **6.** 972
7. 9 boats; 2 soldiers

Part 2, A Division Timeline. pp. 35-36: **1.** 225 tubes   **2.** 16 in.; 18 in.   **3.** Yes
4. 88 votes   **5.** 68 R8
p. 37: **1.** 63 ducats   **2.** 1 writer   **3.** Yes   **4.** 121 votes   **5.** 33 R3   **6.** dividend: 522;
divisor: 6   **7.** dividend: 344; divisor: 8

Division True or False, p. 40: 1. 6   2. 5 R2   3. 5 R6   4. 24   5. 9 R6   6. 4 R3   7. 27   8. 21 R24   9. 11 R6   10. 16 R22   11. 34 R7   12. 7 R29   13. 11   14. 25 R27   15. 3 R54   16. 5 R28   17. 6 R13   18. 7 R14   19. 8 R6   20. 21 R30   21. 21 problems   22. 15 problems   23. 32 miles

What Dogs Want, p. 43: 1. 6   2. 5   3. 4   4. 8   5. 13   6. 52   7. 26   8. 24   9. 26 R17   10. 56   11. 13 R17   12. 17 R31   13. 43   14. 53   15. 57   16. 71   17. 57 R54   18. 103 R41   19. 135 R17   20. 46 R54   21. 16 bones   22. 17 days   23. 3 months

Election 2004, pp. 44-45: 1. 31 packets   2. 4 extra squirts   3. 6 people   4. 4,000 signatures   5. 30 mm   6. 102 votes

p. 46: 1. 42 problems   2. 54 problems   3. 58 problems, with 8 problems left over   4. 6 spider monsters; each monster would solve 126 problems.

Are We Running Out of Jokes?, pp. 47-48: 1. 26,000 jokes; 32,000 jokes; 6,000 jokes lost   2. 17 years   3. about 3 years

p. 49: 1. smaller; 5,000 jokes lost each year   2. increase it to 34 years   3. It would still shrink because more jokes were being used than created.   4. It would last about 102 years.   5. It would grow because no jokes were being used anymore.   6. 51 years

Mental Man, p. 50-51: 8, 10, 12, 15, 27;   30, 300;   50, 500;   6, 60, 600;   9, 9, 90

p. 52: 1. 5, 5, 50   2. 3, 3, 30   3. 6, 6, 60   4. 7, 7, 70   5. 6, 6, 60   6. 5, 5, 50   7. and 8. Possible answer: Cancel out the zeros in the divisor and the dividend and then divide.

Martha Bussell Selects the Best Numbers, pp. 53-54: Possible answers: 76, 78, 80, 82; 78; 555, 855; 855

p. 55: 1. 444, 888   2. 180, 270, 360, 450, 540, 630, 720, 810, 900, 990

Future Gum, pp. 56-57: 8 pieces

p. 58: 1. 60 packs   2. 24 packs   3. 8   4. 15   5. 20   6. 60   7. 20   8. 20   9. 16   10. 36   11. 11   12. 24   13. 26   14. 23   15. 13   16. 25   17. 30   18. 13   19. 16   20. 36   21. 16   22. 25   23. 36   24. 90   25. 100   26. 132

Dirt, p. 60: 4.7 oz; 0.6 million; $7.30; 16.24 mi

p. 61: 0.76 kg; 3.18 oz, 8.48 oz   1. 2.4   2. 0.5   3. 0.61   4. 1.2   5. 4.7   6. 2.43   7. 6.06   8. 63.45   9. 2.7   10. 1.4   11. 4.38   12. 13.47

The Annoying Dragon, p. 64: 1. 82   2. 630   3. 58.3   4. 890   5. 40.3   6. 21   7. 34.3   8. 66   9. 8   10. 562   11. 16   12. 5.3   13. 51.2   14. 62.8   15. 403   16. 6.2   17. 71.4   18. 34.3   19. 65   20. 54.6   21. 530   22. 48   23. 19   24. 196

Martha Bussell's Mathematical Household Hints, p. 66: Explanations may vary. 1. 6 pages; whole numbers   2. $2\frac{2}{5}$; fractions   3. 0.45 oz; decimals   4. $2\frac{2}{3}$ minutes or 2 minutes 40 seconds; fractions   5. 3 R2; need 4 limos; whole numbers   6. 12.86 oz; decimals   7. $1.60; decimals   8. $46.25; decimals

Whopper, p. 67: 110 lies; 10 pages; 61 times; $14.60

p. 68: 1. 23 mpg   2. 2.5 hrs   3. 80 lies   4. 65 nuts

Great Achievement, p. 69: 1. 3 haircuts, 4 shaves   2. 7.68 in.   3. on day 60

p. 70: 1. 7 bad hair days   2. Bad Hair Days—Jan., March, April, June, Aug., Oct., Dec. 3. 3,750 soldiers   4. 4 days   5. 6.4 days   6. 2 days